1

QUEENS SEE QUEENS

QUEENS SEE QUEENS
31 Days of Reflection

Queen,

I wanted to write something that would help us see-

See the best in ourselves, for ourselves.

And, see the best in others, for others..

You are amazing in the most meaningful ways.

Seriously, women are the stuff that incredible is made of-

Daddy God really, really did His thing when He made us.

The world lies when it tells you different.

You lie, when you tell you different.

And perhaps we've rehearsed the lie for so long

that some of us have lost our way.

No worries, I got you.

This daily dose of all things queen will do us good.

Let's Read. Reflect. Repeat.

Let's do it all over again!

DRGENALYN

Gena L. Jerkins, Ed. D

ACKNOWLEDGMENTS

Many thanks to the countless women who are the inspiration behind

this work. Your stories, filled with struggles and successes,

generate awe and admiration deep within my soul.

I am proud of women.

I champion us.

I believe that we are

often the best part of glory untold.

I honor the greatness in you.

Lena Ayeley

Again, thank you for your eyes that carefully read, process, and

give insightful feedback to pages that will touch the lives of many.

Thank you also for eyes that have long seen me and supported

endeavors that represent the best parts of my being.

Queen, I honor the greatness in you.

DEDICATION

Lady Stephanie Nellons-Paige
Thank you for your priceless lessons
on self-worth and self-acceptance,
For years, you have empowered us to shine our brightest lights.

Her: There's something about you that I just don't like.

Lady SNP: No, there is something about yourself that you just don't like. There is something about me that you love. Learn to see yourself better then you will see me and everyone else better.

QUEENS SEE QUEENS

AUTHOR'S NOTE

I see you, queen.

Women are beyond comparison! Although the world often does not cheer when it sees you coming, queen, we are over here clapping it up to acknowledge your arrival. We not only see you coming; We honor you for doing so!

This daily read is written as a marriage of historical snippets, reflective probes, and biblical cross-references. The aim of this piece is to further strengthen a woman's understanding of the wells of value, grace, honor and strength lodged deep within herself. To glean a more exhaustive historical reference, further research into the lives of queens beyond the scope of this book is encouraged.

By gathering insights from the lives of queens through multiple vantage points, may each woman find herself inspired, informed, and challenged by this reflective glimpse into the tapestry of ourselves.

Indulge in 31 days of empowering times of reflection. Then do it all over again.

I see you Queen.

QUEENS SEE QUEENS.

INTRODUCTION

I looked deep inside of me,

Probing within and from the core of me.

With my whole self I searched,

And therein found the best of us.

Passed down through lineage spiritually.

Impacting psyches mentally.

Transcending barriers culturally.

Blazing inroads politically.

Leaving imprints historically.

Wrapped and cloaked ancestrally,

As nothing other than Queens.

I am settling into the ambience of Queens.

A landscape that colors the lens of my perception.

In a myriad of faces, I see queens.

Up close and far beyond,

Queens are both plenteous and rare.

Existing in the nooks and crannies,

Of all that I see and all that I am.

Queens are composed, yet colorful.

Displaying vibrant hues in bold array.

Dignified, yet at times teetering.

On the edge of depression and desperation.

Some reigning, but not ruling, as a shell of a people.

Purpose undefined, denied, pretty faces on display.

Many gloriously victorious,

While death swallowed others early and empty.

Whether courage accompanies them or fades,

Some never reach their full capacity.

Some Queens afraid yet doing it anyway.

Other Queens no longer fearful!

Queens.

Queens are visionaries, relentless adventurers,

Celebrated and executed, demure while revolutionary.

Established in notoriety, reputed infamously.

Other Queens are steady and stoic,

Hovering close as permanent pillars of society,

Of their community, lifelines within their families.

Queens ache while standing, cheer while crying.

Generous and kind-hearted,

Yet fierce and unyielding under pressure.

Queens exist in the box, out of the box.

They create the box, crack ceilings,

Yet establish boundaries and borders,

To give their worlds order.

Queens.

The stories of Queens are the tapestry of us,
The stuff of which women are made.
Enthroned or throneless, more than a woman.
Postured in a tangible place to sit.
Queen is a space where our voices stand,
Our dreams dance, and the universe aligns.
With the royalty that runs in our veins.

I now understand that the study of Queens,
Is an introspective study of me, a study of ourselves.
While standing on the shoulders of those before us,
We also lock elbows with those all around us.
Queens.

For it is not the title of Queen that makes a woman.
It is the quality of a woman that makes a Queen.
The more Queens I study,
The more Queens I see.
I see you Queen.

QUEENS SEE QUEENS.

READ.

REFLECT.

REPEAT.

DAY 1: GOODBYE WISHBONE. HELLO BACKBONE.

Insights from Isabella, Queen of Castile; 1474 A.D

Today's Affirmation: Today, I take on strength to claim what is already mine. I take on courage to withstand even the closest of enemies who may attempt to challenge my rightful access to what is due me. I will not settle for less than all that rightfully belongs to me.

Scripture: For I am the Lord your God who takes hold of your right hand and says to you, do not fear; I will help you. *Isaiah 41:13*

Certainly, it did not come without a fight, but Queen Isabella was here for it all! On that one sentence alone, some of us can already relate! Like Queen Isabella, you know what it is means to have to get with it behind what is rightfully yours. She held on to her right to sit on the throne of Castile despite the odds that were stacked against her.

Prior to Queen Isabella taking her royal seat, the reigning king, her half-brother, attempted to snatch her royalty status. He arrogantly claimed that Isabella had shown disobedience to him by marrying the husband of her choice without his permission. Using this as illegitimate justification, he plotted to block Isabella's claim to the throne. Real quick, do you understand? Has anyone ever tried to block your way to success? Has anyone ever intentionally tried to make your path forward difficult? Queen Isabella took a hard stand against her own blood, her own brother and claimed her proper seat.

She absolutely refused to concede what rightfully belonged to her even at the cost of an estranged relationship with family. Queen, you may know or not know…sometimes others do not like it when you learn to stand up for yourself. Keep standing!

After taking the throne, Queen Isabella's demonstrated that she understood the assignment! Her accomplishments included the reorganization of the governmental system, a decreased crime rate reflecting the lowest her country had experienced in years, and a debt reduction campaign that reversed the negative financial impact of her brother's imbalanced leadership on the kingdom. Additionally, Queen Isabella I underwrote the cost of explorations well beyond the boundaries of her kingdom. She embraced the notion of expanded borders. In the spirit of one of my mentor-girlfriends who often declares over herself, "I am too global to be local."

Indeed, Queen Isabella recognized the value of standing up for herself. As such, she did not sit around wishing that things were different for women in her day, she made things different. Somebody say it with me, "Goodbye wishbone. Hello backbone." She unapologetically insisted on what rightfully belonged to her during a time when women were largely expected to keep silent. She was willing to withstand the pushback, even among family, to obtain her due portion When obstacles attempted to challenge her access to that which she deserved, the queen was relentless in demanding that she have nothing less than what was rightfully hers!

Reflection: Queen Isabella , with an applaudable backbone of fortitude, stood her ground. Like Queen Isabella, do you also need to stand up for something that rightfully belongs to you? Does the promotion, the acknowledgment, financial increase or peace of mind belong to you? Have you allowed less to become your norm? Have you examined why you do so?

Note to
self ~

DAY 2: NOBODY'S SUBSTITUTE
Insights from Hatshepsut, Queen of Egypt; 1473 B.C.

Today's Affirmation: I center myself in peace today. My emotions are anchored. My thoughts are settled. My heart is fixed. Nothing external will disturb the internal peace that is ruling in my life today.

Scripture: You will keep him in perfect peace, whose mind is stayed on You, because he trusts in You. *Isaiah 26:3*

After her father's death, Hatshepsat married her half-brother Thutmose II. Before we go one step further, let's acknowledge for this probable Daddy's girl, this paternal loss was possibly quite crushing. Shortly and suddenly thereafter, 12-year-old Hatshepsut experienced another major life moment. Death decided to visit her doorstep again. After her husband, King Thutmose, died, this young queen found herself widowed and ruling alone. Only twelve years of age, the loss of her Father, queen, the spotlight, married somewhere up in there, and the hubby dies too! Whew chile, we know that sis probably needed a real good nap!

Quite unusual for her time and country, rare circumstances left Queen Hatshepsut as a woman in the position of sole ruler. She was originally meant, according to customary practices, to serve only until her infant stepson was of age to take the throne. But listen, we will fondly call her Queen H 'cause we give nicknames to the inner circle, Queen H debunked the normal practice of serving as only a substitute until the traditional or preferred person could lead. Instead, Queen H took the lead role and served an additional 7 years before taking full reign of the throne in Egypt. She was the third woman to become an Egyptian pharaoh in over 3,000 years of history.

With full awareness that a female serving as a pharaoh was frowned upon, Queen Hatshepsut refused to allow others to minimize her ability to reign. She stepped up to her position and excelled in establishing trade and major building projects for her kingdom. Most importantly, while conflict in opposition to her throne whirled throughout the kingdom, her era was still characterized as a peaceful one. Queen Hatshepsut brought a sense of serenity regardless of the undercurrent of chaos that ran throughout the troubled region. Somehow, in the midst of it all, she settled into being the star not the substitute and reigned with undisturbed inner peace. How about that! That star of your own show, your own life and the peace part should resonate with each of us. That's goals y'all-straight goals!

Reflection: Queen Hatshepsut shut protocol all the way down by refusing to play substitute to another person. I am over here clapping for our girl! Listen queen, have you made that same decision? While you do not have to be front and center in someone else's life, are you committed to certainly being front and center in your own?

Did you underline this emphasis point too? Regardless of the external chaos all around her, Queen Hatshepsut's reign was characterized as a peaceful one. There is something to be said about a queen who does not allow external chaos to impact the internal solitude that she embodies. Talk to me queen, what safeguards do you have in place to ensure that external chaos does not disturb your inner peace?

Note to self ~

DAY 3: R.E.S.P.E.C.T!
Insights from Cleopatra VII, Pharaoh of Ptolemaic Kingdom of Egypt; Near 51 B.C.

Today's Affirmation: Today, I fully embrace the best parts of myself and present them boldly to the world. I also choose to take a break when needed to nourish my best self, safeguarding it from the world. Self-care is a precious priority.

Scripture: I will praise You, for I am fearfully and wonderfully made. *Psalm 139:14*

Considering that the Egyptian throne became her inheritance at the age of 18, Cleopatra evolved into womanhood and a queen at the same time right before the eyes of the public! Now, if you know like I know, 18 years of age would not have been my most desired year to have my whole life played out in the spotlight. So hats off to her because with time, Queen Cleopatra found her stride and transitioned from being co-ruler with family members to being the last independent female ruler of Egypt. During her reign, several major accomplishments included the mitigation of her country's bankruptcy, the establishment of alliances that unified her nation, and the leading of her kingdom's naval fleet into victorious battle.

Now, as if that wasn't enough, it is important to know that Queen Cleopatra was also heralded as one of the richest, shrewdest, and most intelligent women in history. She spoke upwards of ten languages, was educated in mathematics, philosophy, oratory and astronomy. Researchers claim that Cleopatra held her own among the highest ranks of intellectuals and renown scholars worldwide. Renowned for her beauty, Queen Cleopatra went through great effort to highlight her ability to lead over just the appeal of her physique. While, her male cohorts often only emphasized the latter, she demanded a bit more respect!

As Queen Cleopatra lead her country, squabbles with family, rumors about lovers, jealous enemies and factions throughout the kingdom eventually took their toll on her. As a result, her mental wellness, her emotional stability, and soon thereafter, her very zeal to live spiraled downward. Locked away in a palace room, Queen Cleopatra tragically ended her own life. After sacrificially giving over 30 years of giving herself to others, she left very little in reserve to help herself when she needed it the most. And that right there, that is a whole lesson all by itself.

Reflection: Beyond skin deep, beyond what others think, Queen, what are the attributes that you deem most valuable about yourself? See, like Queen Cleopatra, you have to know what you respect most about yourself.

Next up, how do you create opportunity for your best self to show up at the table? All of the men wanted to relegate her to just a pretty face, Queen Cleopatra made room for her intellect, skill set, accomplishments and more to be a part of the dialogue. She determined what they would have to respect to engage her.

Perhaps most importantly, how do you restore your best self so that, unlike Queen Cleopatra, you won't find yourself depleted to the point of self-destruction? Queen, are you reserving a bit of you for you?

Note to self ~

I AM
VALUABLE
BEYOND
MEASURE.

THE

GREATNESS

IN ME

IS HONORED.

DAY 4: A ROCK THAT BENDS TO NO WIND

Insights from Queen Elizabeth I, England; 1558

Today's Affirmation: Today, I have the timing of my blessing settled in my soul. All that is for me is mine. No enemy, distraction, nor obstacle will stop the flow of all that is good for me from coming to me. I will know in full what I have only previously experienced in measure. Amen.

Scripture: No weapon formed against you shall prosper, and every tongue which rises against you in judgment You shall condemn. *Isaiah 54:17*

"Though the sex to which I belong is considered weak, you will nevertheless find me as a rock that bends to no wind," she is quoted as saying.

Queen Elizabeth I's path to the throne was inarguably not easy. Her father, King Henry VIII, annulled his marriage to her mother. With this annulment, Elizabeth's status switched to that of an illegitimate child. As such, she was supposed to be deleted as a successor to the throne. Yes, you're tracking accurately. Her daddy made a decision to leave her mama and just like that, due to no actions of her own, Elizabeth's whole life path was set to change. The way other people's choices can shift stuff in our own lives…don't even me get started!

Although the right to the throne was later returned to her, it could not remove the scars of battle that she ensued while navigating the journey to her rightful inheritance. Queen Elizabeth I paid a cost to get to the throne where she belonged! Here's a quick snippet of what that price looked like-

After the death of her father, her half-sister, Queen Mary, harbored ill intentions toward the rightful heiress and treated her with undeserved cruelty. You see, Mary was just straight up worried that Elizabeth would claim her right to reign. Go figure! So, Mary placed Liz under constant surveillance like she was doing something wrong. For a period, she even sequestered Elizabeth in isolation. As a quick side note, right here is a great place to remind us that offen people's ill treatment of you is not about something that you have done to them but rather a reflection of their heart or actions toward you.

When Mary's harsh treatment escalated to death threats, Elizabeth, did her best to avoid doing anything that might have been used as grounds for her own execution. Ever been there, working hard to be on the friendly side of someone who means you no good? At the end of the day, well actually all day, Elizabeth simply could not resolve Mary's internal conflict. For us too, someone else's inner resolution is not our responsibility to carry.

When Mary died, Elizabeth became one of England's most influential monarchs. With the Elizabethan Age as a namesake, Queen Elizabeth

I's rule postured England as a major powerhouse in politics, commerce, and arts. Queen Elizabeth literally defined an era.

Reflection: Although delayed, Elizabeth I eventually took her rightful place as Queen of England. We can only imagine the wisdom and patience required to navigate the path to the throne among the enemy. Do you need laser sharp wisdom or perhaps a calm spirit to determine how to move forward in a specific area in the face of adversity? God's wisdom is available to you Queen. Say it with me," I receive Daddy's God incomparable wisdom for each part of my today!"

Note to
self ~

DAY 5: NEVERMIND, NEXT, NOW.
Insights from Queen Elizabeth II, England; 1952

Today's Affirmation: Today, I declare limitless thinking regarding my own potential. Against any odds, I challenge myself to move forward with intentionality. I am encouraged to obtain all that is purposeful for my life. I can win simply because I CAN WIN!

Scripture: I can do all things through Christ who strengthens me. *Philippians 4:13*

During her grandfather's reign, Elizabeth was third in the line of succession to potentially sit on the throne. Both her uncle and father preceded her. Although her birth generated a small ripple of public interest, she was not expected to ever become queen.

When her grandfather died, Elizabeth's Uncle Edward sat on the throne. True to royal practice, his entire lineage was the predestined heirs to the throne. Suddenly though, good ole' Uncle abdicated the throne so that he could marry the love of his life (that's another story for a different day). That one decision made Elizabeth's father the new reigning king. With the lineage of heirship switching instantly, Elizabeth, as eldest child to her father, transitioned from "not likely" to "next in line" to sit in that royal seat!

Around 1952, after her father died, at the young age of 18 years old, Queen Elizabeth II was crowned the new queen of her country.

Imagine that trajectory, from "not likely" to "next in line" to NOW! That small ripple at birth just swelled into a roaring wave.

For us too queen, it can certainly happen. Just like that, Queen Elizabeth became. head of the Commonwealth. **Additionally, she because queen regnant** of seven independent Commonwealth countries. To date (2022), she is currently the longest living and longest reigning British monarch. Queen Elizabeth also carries the title of the world's longest-serving female head of state. From that never mind status, given that she was a girl and not of the right lineage, Queen Elizabeth suddenly landed in her now! Queen, will you declare it with me? "I am shifting from nevermind to next...to right now!"

Reflection: With the odds stacked squarely against her, Queen Elizabeth II transitioned into rulership on the throne of England. She went from least likely to literally next in line to leading a kingdom NOW! Please consider, perhaps there are areas where you are minimizing your aptitude to succeed because the odds are seemingly stacked against you. Is it possible that regardless of the obstacles, you can amd you will transition to "next in line"? Are you willing to accept sudden and short transitions that shift your entire life from next to your now?

Note to
self ~

WHAT GOD HAS FOR ME IS FOR ME.

I AM WHOLE.

NOTHING MISSING.

NOTHING BROKEN.

DAY 6: ABUNDANCE TOO SOON

Insights from Queen Mary, Scotland; 1542

Today's Affirmation: Today, my mental capabilities are strong and becoming more sharpened by the people that You have given for my life. Timing and preparation will equip me to meet my destiny. I will submit to the process of preparation so that I may experience the benefits of being ready for all that God has ordained for my life.

Scripture: Study diligently to present yourself approved to God; a worker who does not need to be ashamed. *2 Timothy 2:15*

Now this snippet right here makes me desire that each and all of us have trusted mentors that can pull our coattails and help us to get it all the way together! In a recent promotion opportunity, one of mine certainly tapped my shoulder and without minced words helped me to know that my performance was lacking. "Quite frankly," she said, "I was embarrassed." As for that assessment right there, I guarantee, it never happened again. The details of that scenario are for another day. Let's lean into Queen Mary for a moment together.

As the only surviving legitimate child of King James V of Scotland, Mary, Queen of Scotland, ascended to the throne at the mere age of six days old! Talking about being on a fast track, this queen shot years ahead of her time. Because of her young age, regents were appointed to rule the nation until she became an adult. Although she lacked trusted guidance, when she came of age, Mary was crowned to sit on the throne.

Queen Mary's rule in Scotland was plagued by scandal early on in her tutelage. Perhaps searching for that missing piece of a father figure, she married and endured the loss of two husbands, one by an untimely death and the second by murder. The general public actually believed that Queen Mary's third husband had a hand in the death of the former. There was an uprising against the couple when Mary later married him. As a result, Mary was imprisoned. Years later, she was forced to vacate the throne.

Some time later, after an unsuccessful attempt to regain the throne, Mary fled southward seeking the protection of her family, Queen Elizabeth I of England. Regardless of past tensions, Mary was hopeful for a place of reprieve and comfort. Perceiving Mary as a threat, Elizabeth had her confined in various castles and manor houses. After eighteen and a half years in custody, Mary was found guilty of plotting to assassinate Elizabeth. She was beheaded in the following year. In Queen Mary's case, it is believed that the lack of guidance, combined with abundance too soon, with no preparation, wounded her more than advanced her life.

Reflection: Queen Mary's ill fate is largely associated with a lack of preparation for her position. Queen, are you adequately preparing for your aspirations? Unlike Queen Mary, have you secured mentors who can perhaps fill voids and provide guidance in your personal and professional development? Sis, we can not be too proud or self-sufficient to submit ourselves to someone who is farther up the road than us.

Note to
self ~

Day 7: I'M GOOD WITH "ONLY"

Insights from Queen Marie Theresa, Austria; 1747

Today's Affirmation: Today I declare that I live greatly. The rest of my days will be filled with advancement and progression. I will defy odds/expectations and any negative word of failure spoken over me. I will cultivate character that aligns with my greatness. I will excel bountifully.

Scripture: It is God who arms me with strength for today and makes my way perfect. *Psalms 18: 32*

In her day, Queen Maria Theresa of Austria was the only woman to rule over the Habsburg dominions of the Holy Roman Empire. She served with quiet commitment as sovereign of the countries of Austria, Hungary, Croatia, Bohemia,   Transylvania,   Mantua, Milan, Galicia, the Austrian Netherlands, and Parma. Yes! This queen stepped up to the plate and had no qualms with being the only female ruling influencer in the territory.

Queen Maria Theresa defied most expectations. With little training to rule, she still reigned decades on the throne. During this time, she strengthened her impoverished empire's international standing by building up military forces, improving the education system for her country, as well as developing the commercial industry within her vast kingdom. With little experience on her resume", what was her saving grace to ruling successfully?   Queen Maria utilized Enlightened

Absolutism as her philosophical model, she strengthened her authority by improving the lives of her nation's subjects. In short, she lead well within her kingdom by serving her people well.

Contrastingly, this is also where Queen Maria Theresa got herself in trouble. Although she loved her own people well, she allowed personal prejudices to guide her treatment of other nationalities. She despised the Jews and the Protestants. On certain occasions, she ordered their expulsion to remote parts of the realm. A queen with such large intellectual capabilities still operated small-mindedly when it came to embracing those who were different from her own ethnicity. Man, may we examine ourselves Queen! May we see the areas where we need to improve in our ability to treat others with dignity regardless of their ethnicity, financial levels, social status, etc. I know for certain, it was more difficult for someone to get an appointment with me as school principal after mistreating my front desk assistant because her title/position was different than mine. How we treat others who we view as different is quite critical.

Reflection: Queen Maria Theresa defied the odds and forged new paths of success for herself. Someone else's devaluation of her potential did not deter her from charting her own path. And you Queen, are you setting your own way for your life? Are you good with being the only one like you who may be mastering your particular skillset?

Let's also examine areas that should be adjusted in our character so that greatness does not fall through our cracks as a result of our own overlooked, tolerated, or justified shortcomings.

Note to
self ~

ALWAYS
REMEMBER,
YOU'VE GOT
REASONS
TO HOLD YOUR
HEAD HIGH
QUEEN.

QUEEN, YOU ARE THE ANSWER TO SOMEBODY'S PRAYER.

DAY 8: NOTHING OF INTEREST

Insights from Catherine The Great, Russia; 1762

Today's Affirmation: I have nothing missing. I have nothing broken. Again, I have nothing missing. I have nothing broken. (Repeat)

Scripture: And He said to me, "My grace is sufficient for you, for My strength is made perfect in weakness." *2 Corinthians 12:9*

They tried to discredit her but it would not work. If you don't catch anything else, catch that queen!

Catherine the Great of Russia rose from a low-level German princess to a celebrated yet scandalized Russian Empress. By her own admission, Catherine's childhood was quite uneventful as she once expressed in a letter: "I see nothing of interest in it." Ironically interesting, that eventless period of childhood morphed into the reign of one the country's longest-ruling female leader.

Listen, here's the tea on our queen-sister Queen Catherine. She came to power after a self-initiated coup which overthrew her husband. With her successful acquisition of new territory, introduction of new religious and educational reforms, she escorted Russia into the mainstage of European power.

Most renown, bravely driving down a controversial road during her time, Queen Catherine the Great unabashedly decided to trailblaze and have not only herself, but also her son, inoculated against smallpox. In fact, she desired to have vaccinations given to her countrymen throughout her entire empire. By the 1800s, approximately two-million inoculations had been administered in the Russian Empire. The period of Catherine the Great's rule, the Catherinian Era, is considered the Golden Age of Russia.

Regardless of all of her wins, wanting to see her reign reduced by ridicule, it is believed that some spread persistent rumors regarding her love life. These ugly tales were commonly reputed as staged to discredit and highlight her unfitness to rule. While they mocked, completely manipulated, scorned, and enacted numerous efforts to undermine her success, Queen Catherine is recounted in history as one of the most influential Russian leaders to have ever reigned.

Reflection: Neither her childhood nor bloodline set her up for any spectacular sort of head start; yet Queen Catherine contributed quite significantly and is revered to this day throughout her country. May we too embrace that our beginnings do not determine our endings. If there was a deficit in our early years, may His grace be sufficient to meet our every need.

Note to
self ~

DAY 9: WHEN WE KNOW BETTER-
Insights from Queen Anne Boleyn of England; 1526

Today's Affirmation: I will walk in wisdom, choose with depth in my understanding, and act with discernment, redeeming time that has already been wasted. I will progress with purpose by heeding my lessons learned.

Scripture: Who is wise and understanding among you? Let him show by good conduct that his works are done in the meekness of wisdom. *James 3:13*

With no intentions of her own, Anne Boleyn caught the eye of King Henry VIII. In other words, she was minding her own business when the King made her his business. Although it was common in her day for a king to have multiple love interests, Anne resisted his pursuit, refusing to become one of his mistresses. For her hand in marriage, King Henry broke from the Catholic Church, as they would not condone a termination of marriage. He divorced his wife, and pursued Anne even more obstinately.

Her first mind was to resist him because she personally witnessed the king's ability to manipulate circumstances to get his desired results. Anne later went against her gut and the waving red flags. She agreed to his proposal. Anne can move over and let some of us slide into her shoes right here. I know that she's not the first one of us to go against our guts! SMH, God help us!

Shortly after the nuptials, the Pope of the Catholic Church decreed sentences of punishment against King Henry. As a result of his new marriage to Queen Anne and resulting excommunication, the first break between the Church of England and the Roman Catholic Church took place.

The Church of England was brought under King Henry's control. Anne was crowned Queen of England and gave birth to their first heiress a few months later. Things appeared to be going well between the couple until that birth. Given he already had six daughters with his first wife, an eager King Henry was disappointed when his newest spouse birth yet another daughter. He hoped with subsequent tries that a boy would soon follow.

Anne tried repeatedly to produce the coveted son but failed. She endured three miscarriages in the process. True to form, Henry VIII started to court another woman and to seek a divorce. He had Anne investigated for high treason. Regrettably, the screams of her gut had been ignored. As the King moved on to his number next, Queen Anne was tried before a jury of her peers and beheaded four days later under the crime of treason..

Reflection: For Queen Anne, the red flags were all around highlighting the character flaws of her future husband; yet, she married him. She had watched him display the same tendencies with others that he eventually used to take her life. Queens, with no judgment whatsoever, we have to stand in our own truth about various situations in our lives.

Like Queen Anne, are there decisions we have made which steamrolled past the red flags all around us? I certainly can name a few moments of could have, should have, would have...

Queen, are we choosing differently now as a part of our lessons learned? One of my girlfriends would often quote, "When we know better, we do better." We should anyways for, that is where the redemption lies.

Note to
self ~

DAY 10: MANY TITLES

Insights from Queen Nefertiti, Egypt; Nineteenth Dynasty

Today's Affirmation: I grant myself permission to evolve, grow, expand, and shift. I willingly embrace the various expressions of myself. I flow with the exploration of all that my heart desires to accomplish.

Scripture: I will praise You, for I am fearfully and wonderfully made; Marvelous are Your works, and that my soul knows very well. *Psalms 139:14*

Nefertiti was promoted to co-regent by her husband before his death. After his passing, she still held it down on the throne! Now that's a particularly rare accomplishment in the land of Egypt. I mean this queen-sister was a bad, bad girl! Unapologetically, she did the absolute most!

Queen Nefertiti is depicted in many archaeological sites as equal in stature to a King. Her accomplishments certainly did not allow anyone to regard her as less than her male counterparts. Her reputation includes destroying Egypt's enemies, brazenly riding a chariot, and worshiping the Aten in the manner of a Pharaoh. Some historians speculate that she may have also ruled as a pharaoh alone. It is likely that Nefertiti, in similar fashion to previous female Pharaohs, assumed the kingship under a male name, physically disguised herself as a male, and assumed the male alter-ego while ruling. She did all of this for the sake of her cohorts who could not accept nor handle female leadership.

Now, here's the clap even harder part - Queen Nefertiti lived out many expressions of herself. Like this woman literally refused to be put in a box. Her multiple titles included:

- Hereditary Princess
- Great of Praises
- Lady of Grace
- Lady of The Two Lands
- Main King's Wife, his beloved
- Great King's Wife, his beloved
- Lady of All Women
- Mistress of Upper & Lower Egypt

A legendary beauty, it is recorded that Queen Nefertiti ruled with more power than most Egyptian queens. Her historical significance was beyond skin deep. She helped to establish a new monotheist religion within the empire. and reigned in what was arguably the wealthiest period of Ancient Egyptian history. Queen Nefertit secured the bag!

Reflection: As indicated by her many titles, Queen Nefertiti lived various expressions of herself. She could not be boxed into one single summary. Like our queen sister, let's continue to explore the fullness of who we are. We are more! Think about it Queen. What other expressions of your greatness still need opportunity to live boldly on display?

Note to
self ~

DAY 11: HISSED AND JEERED

Insights from Queen Victorian, United Kingdom; 1837

Today's Affirmation: I declare that both my character and integrity are uncompromising assets for my life. I safeguard my own well-being by highly regarding the well-being of others. I will ensure that others are well in my care.

Scripture: By this will men know that you are My disciples, by the love that you have for one another. *John 13:35*

Known as the Victorian era, her reign of sixty-three years and seven months was longer than that of any of her predecessors. Queen Victoria's reign was trademarked as a period of progressiveness in cultural identity, evolution is the development of defense tactics, as well as advancement in political arenas for the United Kingdom. In addition, her era was heralded as a time of great expansion for the British Empire.

As part of her legacy, Queen Victoria championed many social reforms to aid the country's growing urban population. She was a unifying symbol for the British Empire, bringing various towns and villages together under one cadence and inspiring hope. Beyond her country, her international connections were steeped heavily with other prominent royals. As a benefit of their mother's widespread influence,

Queen Victoria's nine children, each and every one of them, married into significant ruling monarchies of the era. But then-

At the start of her reign, Queen Victoria was indeed popular. Yet, her reputation began to decline when one of her mother's ladies-in-waiting developed an abdominal growth that was widely rumored to be an out-of-wedlock pregnancy. Queen Victoria believed the rumors and thus treated the accused woman with hatred. Yes, a queen hated another woman based on a rumor! A campaign implicating the Queen for spreading false rumors was extremely detrimental to her reputation and worsened when the lady-in-waiting died from a sickness after being found innocent. At public appearances, Victoria was literally hissed and jeered relentlessly.

Reflection: From princess to overnight successor, Queen Victoria experienced such unusual grace as she transitioned to the throne. Sadly, she did not extend this same measure of grace to another but instead found herself indulging in less than kind behavior. To add insult to injury, the queen's harshness was based on false information. Queen listen, while God's favor can open doors, our own character must help sustain His granted opportunities.

Note to
self ~

QUEEN,
EVEN ON YOUR
WORST DAY,
YOU ARE STILL
VALUABLE.

QUEEN,
EVEN WHILE YOU'RE
WORKING ON WHO YOU
ARE TRYING TO BE,
YOU ARE ALREADY GOOD
ENOUGH!

DAY 12: UNBELOVED

Insights from Queen Marie-Antoinette, France; 1744

Today's Affirmation: Today my business decisions are rooted in proven practices of success and principles of solid stewardship. I will lead with stability, not personal preferences, biases, or dependencies on familiar relationships. I will consistently access if my personal connections are productive for my purpose.

Scripture: Do you see a man who excels in his work? He will stand before kings: He will not stand before unknown men.
Proverbs 22:29

Queen Marie-Antoinette, France's last queen before the French revolution, was declared guilty and condemned to death for robbing the national treasury. Furthermore, her charges included conspiracy accusations against the security of the State and high treason in the interest of the enemy.

Over time, a growing percentage of the population came to dislike her. They accused Queen Marie-Antoinette of being recklessly extravagant and promiscuous with various suitors. Others believed that she held deep loyalties for enemies of France in favor of her homeland, Austria. With ever increasing resentment towards her majesty, "Madame Deficit" became the title of choice by the public for their unbeloved queen. The general population blamed her for the overdrawn condition of France's budget. It was as if it was not enough that she spent wastefully; she also fought all efforts for financial reform within the system.

October 1793, Queen Marie-Antoinette's trial began for her destructive behavior. In just two days, she was convicted of high treason with no mercy from her accusers. In her final hours, she held steadfast to her claim of having a clear conscience, her adherence to Catholicism, and her deep devotion to her offspring. Despite the watching and jeering crowd, Queen Marie-Antoinette maintained her composure while riding in an open cart for the hour it took to reach the guillotine where she was beheaded.

Reflection: It is believed that Queen Marie-Antoinette was indeed guilty of utilizing her throne to benefit family and friends from her native country at the expense of her kingdom. She was accused of leading based on personal preferences and favoritism. Inevitably, the ones for which she sacrificed her all were incapable of contributing anything to help save her. In those connections, she had more to lose than she ever stood to gain. Queen, let's agree on this quick prayer, "God help us to not self-sabotage in the interest of saving others, especially those who can do absolutely nothing in return to save us!"

Note to
self ~

DAY 13: STILL A QUEEN

Insights from Queen Catherine, England; 1509

Today's Affirmation: I shake off the residue of anyone's inability to see my value. I acknowledge that I am worthy of all things good, wonderful, and beautiful. I see me.

Scripture: But you are a chosen generation, a royal priesthood, a holy nation, His own special people, that you may proclaim the praises of Him who called you out of darkness into His marvelous light.
1 Peter 2:8

Catherine, Princess of Wales, was 3 years old when she was betrothed to Arthur, Prince of Wales. Hello betrothed! Yes, they were engaged and then married in 1501, but Arthur died five months later. Subsequently, Catherine became the ambassador of the Aragonite Crown to England in 1507, the first female ambassador in European history.

Eventually, Queen Catherine of Aragon married King Henry VIII, her late husband's younger brother. As such, she became Queen of England. In 1513, she served as regent of England while Henry VIII was in France. During her husband's absence, the English won the critical Battle of Flodden. During this event, Queen Catherine played an important part by giving an emotional speech about English courage, inspiring a nation to be victorious. Sadly, after all that she contributed, her husband would still deem it not enough.

Although the Queen bore him six children, Henry decided to end his marriage to Catherine because she did not birth a male heir for him. At the risk of being ostracized, Queen Catherine would not go along with King Henry's plan that they quietly divorce. She absolutely refused to coverup his foolery.

When King Henry VIII remarried, Queen Catherine considered herself to still be the rightful queen. Against all protocol of those days, when the King, on behalf of his new wife, requested her crown jewels, that request was matched by the ultimate silent treatment. Queen Catherine concluded that although her former husband fraudulently opted to shamelessly dishonor his marriage vows, she would not cosign his efforts. Instead, she refused to part ways with either her castle or crown. She understood that while the King may decided to switch his affections from her to another, sis listen, Queen Catherine knew enough to still value herself! Queen Catherine deemed herself still the queen.

Reflection: There is something to be said about a queen who does not allow tradition, protocol, or someone else to redefine her worth and status. And you Queen, are you vibing her energy? Please understand, others may alter what you mean to them but absolutely no one should have the power to alter the essence of what you mean to yourself.

Note to self ~

DAY 14: LADIES OF NOBILITY

Insights from Queen Eleanor of Aquitaine, Europe; 1137

Today's Affirmation: I declare that my connections will see and know who I am as a person. My essence will be captured with more significance than my success and/or attributes. My personhood is a priority. I will maintain myself, my core, my center – all things that make me well. I see me.

Scripture: One who has unreliable friends soon comes to ruin, but there is a friend who sticks closer than a brother. *Proverbs 18:24*

Queen Eleanor of Aquitaine was one of the wealthiest and most powerful women in western Europe during the High Middle Ages. Inheriting a vast estate at the age of only 15 made her the most sought-after bride of her generation. She would eventually become the queen of France, the queen of England and lead a crusade to the Holy Land.

Queen Eleanor of Aquitaine, overwhelmed by the brutal Parisian cold versus the warmth of southern France, is credited with introducing built-in fireplaces to the kingdom. Eleanor's innovation spread quickly, transforming the domestic arrangements of that time period. Yes to women throughout the kingdom sitting fireside in their homes! Long before women's suffrage was a movement, Queen Eleanor was utilizing her throne to impact the lives of ladies in her kingdom.

Of interest also, sources praise Eleanor's beauty. Even in an era when ladies of the nobility were excessively praised, their praise of her was undoubtedly enlarged beyond compare. In her youth, she was described as more than beautiful. When she was around 30, she was called "gracious, lovely, the embodiment of charm," extolled for her "lovely eyes and noble countenance" and declared as worthy to be on the arm of any King. Even in her old age, Queen Eleanor was described as beautiful. Despite all these words of praise, no one left a more detailed description of Eleanor. Common features such as the color of her hair and shade of eyes, for example, are unknown. Character reflections, insights on her dreams, aspirations, additional noteworthy accomplishments are all noticeably missing from her records. In many ways, she was a highly visible, invisible being.

Reflection: It is recorded that others did not see Queen Eleanor beyond skin-deep. With all of her attributes and possible accomplishments, researchers note that no one really depicted her with details beyond generic renderings of her physical features. Have you ever longed to be visible, a yearning for more to validate your presence? I see you queen.

Note to self ~

UNAPOLOGETICALLY, LISTEN TO YOUR SOUL.

QUEEN,
MAY YOU TASTE IN FULL
WHAT YOU HAVE ONLY
KNOWN IN MEASURE.

DAY 15: MEAGER BEGINNINGS

Insights from Queen Theodora, Eastern Roman; 527

Today's Affirmation: Afraid or not, fear will not stop my voice. With full boldness or knees buckling, I will move forward regardless with full expression of all that I am. My valuable voice deserves to be heard.

Scripture: So do not fear, for I am with you; do not be dismayed, for I am your God. I will strengthen you and help you; I will uphold you with my righteous right hand. *Isaiah 43:13*

Empress Theodora was born as part into the peasant class, to a father who was a bear trainer. After his death, her mother, unable to support her three children, placed she and her sisters into society as "actresses", an activity that was banned by the church. Justinian, nephew of the Emperor, saw the beautiful Theodora at a show and fell deeply in love with her. He persuaded his uncle to repeal the Roman law prohibiting marriage of the great officers of the empire to "actresses". Absolutely, he changed the law to secure her love!

Although from meager beginnings, Empress Theodora is remembered as one of the most powerful women in Byzantine history. She used her power and influence to promote religious and social policies. She was one of the first rulers to recognize the rights of women, passing strict laws to prohibit the trafficking of young girls and altering the divorce laws to give greater benefits to women.

Theodora proved to be a worthy and able leader during the Nika riots as well. There were two rival political factions in the Empire who set many public buildings on fire and proclaimed a new emperor. Unable to control the mob, Justinian and his officials prepared to run. At a meeting, Theodora interrupted them claiming: "My lords, the present occasion is too serious to allow me to follow the convention that a woman should not speak in a man's council." Her speech convinced them all to fight and win. Later, they went on to rebuild and reform Constantinople and made it the most splendid city the world had seen for centuries. Undoubtedly, here's a queen who understood the value of her voice, her contribution, thoughts and perspectives.

Reflection: Queen Theodora broke restrictive protocol and became the voice of reason and hope during a tumultuous time. She understood the unmatched value of her words, the power in her wisdom, insight, and thoughts that she brought to a situation. Queens, may her courageousness inspire us as we continue to honor the voice within us.

Note to
self ~

DAY 16: BREAK PRECEDENT

Insights from Queen Wu Zetian, Tang Dynasty; 665

Today's Affirmation: In my desire to excel, I understand that I am in this world but not of it. In my pursuit of success, may my actions represent God's Kingdom with an exceptional standard of excellence. Whether I deem it karma or reaping what I have sown, may I contribute good to the world and receive goodness and mercy in return, all my days.

Scripture: So may the words of my mouth, my meditation, thoughts, and every movement of my heart be always pure and pleasing, acceptable before your eyes, my only God. *Psalms 19:14*

For twenty-five years, Wu Zetian served as co-ruler alongside her husband and sons. For an additional 15 years, she was the only officially recognized empress regent of China in more than two millennia. Wu Zetian's extended period of political and military leadership included the major expansion of the Chinese empire, the establishment of important stabilization variables regarding social class in Chinese society, an organized state-wide support for Buddhism, education, and access to literature for all. Queen Wu Zetian broke precedent again when she founded her own Zhou dynasty. Started her own dynasty, yes she did!

Queen Wu was regarded as ruthless in her endeavors to grab power. She was reputed as a power-hungry woman with no care for who she hurt or what she did. For example, one of her own children was killed. Regardless of what caused the death of the child, Wu blamed her rival and had her removed from the position of Empress. Her political ambition outweighed any efforts to truthfully find and prosecute the murderer of her child.

Empress Wu used similar tactics towards those who opposed her ascension. She was infamously reputed for making false accusations, demoting and stripping of titles and authority from competitors, limiting provision and resources, executing permanent exile, house arrest and forced suicide. It was said that during this time, no official dared to criticize the empress. She is renown for demonstrating ruthless leadership to get to her desired end.

Reflection: Do we truly believe that our end justifies the means? Or rather, do we believe that our outcome is only applaudable if the steps which afforded the opportunity are honorable as well. Unlike Queen Wu, may we always understand that wrong winning is not winning at all.

Note to
self ~

DAY 17: LEGENDS ARE MADE

Insights from Queen Kandake, Ethiopia; c. 40 - 10 BC

Today's Affirmation: I survived the struggle that left the scar. My bumps, bruises, and scars are proof of my strength. I am strong, stronger than, AND strong enough.

Scripture: The Lord is my strength and my song; He has given me victory. This is my God, and I will praise him -my father's God, and I will exalt him! *Exodus 15:2*

Queen Kandake was the stuff of which legends are made. She is reputed to have been blind in one eye, having lost it in a battle with the Romans. Yet, she was proudly a woman out on the front lines of her kingdom's heaviest fights. An injury could not stop her. She was known to be a fierce, tactical, and a relentless leader.

Queen Kandake was not only a warrior on the battlefield, defying odds and defeating enemies. She was also a fighter in her personal life. Against the precedent of her day, she was believed to have had her own court. She acted as a landholder, and held a prominent secular role as regent. She refused to succumb to the pre-established norms which boxed in who women could be in that day.

Interestingly, Greek fables and legendary tales frequently reference Queen Kandake as "one-eyed Candace". Of course, such a moniker can be viewed as comical or insulting when the audience does not know the backdrop of her injury. However, the context of the loss of her eye is quite heroic. Her scar was proof of one of her most renown victories. As ugly as the struggle was for her, as painful as the process of accepting the permanent trauma, there is also a depth to her victory that cannot be undermined. Her name, Queen Kandake, from centuries past, is still chronicled in history to this day. They may mock her scar; but she is remembered for her victory!

Reflection: Perhaps, like Queen Kandake, the very thing that seems to be a constant reminder of a difficult time in your life is simultaneously your badge of success. Queen, it is possible that the thing that forever left its imprint on your life strengthens you to leave your mark on this world.

Note to
self ~

DAY 18: A ROYAL LINEAGE

Insights from Meroitic Queens, Egypt; 170 BC - 314 BC

Today's Affirmation: Today, I will not underestimate the power of my impact. Instead, I will embrace the tremendous amount of influence that my presence, my voice, my endorsement carries and wisely use it to empower good in the world.

Scripture: You are the light of the world. A town built on a hill cannot be hidden. *Matthew 5:14*

There were several female rulers of Ethiopia. This area is also known as the ancient Kingdom of Kush. Within this realm, the queens of Meroe, the capital of Kush, went by the dynasty title of Kandake. Some Kandakes ruled alone. Others ruled with their husbands and had equal power with the king.

The iconographic portrayal of the Meroitic queens depicts them as women often alone, in regal clothing and at the forefront of their stelae (upright stone slabs erected in the ancient worlds as monuments) in sculptures. In depictions, a large shawl was wrapped around the queen's body with an additionally decorated cloak worn over the first. The first association with this element of dress is a king's coronation ceremony.

The most important event that the Meroitic queens participated in was kingships; they ensured continuity within their own lineage. Without these regal women, the royal ceremonies for kingship were incomplete. Their influence was undeniable as they navigated factors to ensure that their families, throughout multiple generations, were situated for longevity and optimal success on the throne. In these ceremonial enthronements, the king was even accompanied by female members of his family - mother, and wife. The king's mother's presence played an essential role in the legitimacy of her son as the king. By his side, she represented approval, acceptance, blessed authority, and an endorsement from forefathers who ruled before, a royal passing of the torch.

Reflection: The undeniable impact of the Meroitic queens shaped kingships and dynasties for centuries. While not directly in power, these women used their influence both naturally and spiritually to shape nations. A dear male friend of mine often speaks of the influential power of women to change the trajectory of a circumstance. With time, I have grown to understand that he has tapped into a bit of truth there. May we learn to harness and utilize the power of our influence.

Note to
self ~

DAY 19: GRACIOUS LEADERSHIP
Insights from Queen Candance, Ethiopia; 332 BC

Today's Affirmation: I will lead as I desire to be led. I will seek to build others up and help them to reach their full potential. I am committed to adding value to those around me. May my assuredness in who I am allow me to be confident in lifting and serving others fully. No comparison. No competition.

Scripture: So in everything, do to others what you would have them do to you, for this sums up the Law and the Prophets. *Matthew 7:12*

his is the queen of the Ethiopians whose "eunuch" or chamberlain was converted to Christianity by what is widely believed to be a divinely ordained meeting with Philip the evangelist (Acts 8:27). The eunuch's ability to indulge in literature and lean into his curiosity while traveling on behalf of Queen Candance speaks to her gracious nature and considerate leadership.

Queen Candance ruled the Greeks *Meroe*, in Upper Nubia. This route was central to the commercial trade between Africa and the south of Asia. With the heavy traffic of trade and commerce, this area became known for its abundant wealth and opulent standards of living. Although others coveted her prosperous domain, she was able to sustain her leadership of the area.

Interestingly, Queen Candance maintained her ability to lead while demonstrating kindness to those within her realm, inclusive of her servants. That sense of mature character, the ability to prioritize humanity above position, was probably established within her heart long before the crown was placed on her head.

Reflection: Leadership is reflected in how you treat the least of these. The eunuch, even in a servant position, was empowered to learn, to inquire, to evolve and grow. Confident leaders seek to promote prosperity for those under their care.

Note to
self ~

GIVE
YOURSELF
GRACE
IN BIG
& SMALL
WAYS.

YOU'RE GOLDEN QUEEN.

Day 20: HER LEGACY

Insights from Joanna of Castile, Castile & Aragon; 1516

Today's Affirmation: In the spirit of the serenity prayer, *"God, grant me the serenity to accept the things I cannot change, courage to change the things I can, and wisdom to know the difference,"* - Reinhold Niebuhr.

May I be strengthened to make any necessary changes in my own life to maintain my own peace. While I cannot govern others, God grant me strength to work on me.

Scripture: And the peace of God, which transcends all understanding, will guard your hearts and your minds in Christ Jesus.
Philippians 4:7

Joanna of Castile was queen of both Castile and Aragon. She was described as an intelligent young woman who received an excellent education. She loved to read classical literature, spoke multiple languages inclusive of Castilian, Leonese, Galician–Portuguese, and Catalan along with Latin and French. She had a penchant for canon and civil law, heraldry, grammar, history, mathematics, and philosophy. Joanna also took lessons in good manners, etiquette, dancing, drawing, embroidery, needlepoint, and sewing. She was a talented musician who also hunted.

Although she was the queen of Castile for more than 50 years, with skill sets beyond compare, the tragedy lies in Queen Joanna's legacy. She was infamously known as "Joanna, La Loca" or "Joanna The Mad". She spent most of her leadership years confined due to bouts with insanity. Some believed that she started to show signs of mental instability when her mother died. The majority believed that her mental instability began with her marriage and worsened because of her husband's infidelity. While many speculate regarding the origin of her mental decline, there are no records of meaningful interventions or safe plans that served to help her navigate those dark moments.

The most famous and relevant proof of her mental disorder was revealed when her husband died. After refusing to let go of his embalmed body for an extended period, she finally accepted his death and allowed for his burial. In a change of mind, she later exhumed the body and kept it in her quarters. She would often open his casket so she could embrace and kiss him. In the end, she consented to have him buried again just outside her window.

Reflection: Even a crown cannot replace the priceless value of peace. Queen Joanna, in her brilliance, was relegated to confinement because of mental illness. Her lack of mental peace was largely associated with worry over her husband's behavior, something she could not control or change. Admittedly, there is no judgment here. Even as I write, I reflect on the numerous times I have found myself anxiously stewing over someone's behavior or other matters that are beyond my power to change.

Note to
self ~

DAY 21: COMPARTMENTALIZED CHAOS

Insights from Queen Margaret, France; 1589

Today's Affirmation: Peaceful moments, peace breaks, peaceful thoughts, peaceful spaces, and peaceful company are mine all throughout the day as I intentionally erect boundaries of peace in my own life.

Scripture: You will keep *him* in perfect peace, whose mind *is* stayed *on You, b*ecause he trusts in You. *Isaiah 26:3*

Traditionally for her day, via her father's arrangement, Queen Margaret became engaged to Prince Charles of France. Despite it being an arranged relationship, Margaret developed a genuine affection for her fiancee' Charles. He, on the other hand, renounced the agreement and married Margaret's stepmother. Of course, the unwedded bride was deeply hurt by Charles's action. She was left with a feeling of enduring resentment towards him and his country.

Margaret's second husband, John, died after only six months of marriage. Pregnant with their child, Margaret gave birth to a premature stillborn daughter. Trying again, Margaret married a third time but was left childless and widowed after three years. She possibly felt as if she could never catch a break. The death of her husband compounded with the loss of her child seemed like the unbearable breaking point.

One day, heavy with deep sadness and grief, she threw herself out of a window, in a drastic suicide attempt. Inexplicably, she survived the fall and her life was spared. After being persuaded to bury her husband, she had his heart embalmed so she could keep it with her forever. She became known as the Lady of Mourning.

Despite her heartbreak, Margaret had a remarkably successful career on the throne. She became the only woman elected as ruler by the representative assembly. She negotiated the restoration of a treaty of commerce with England, played a role in the formation of the League of Cambrai, played a crucial role in her nephew's election as Holy Roman Emperor, and was the only regent ever re-appointed indefinitely. Her reign was a period of relative peace and prosperity.

Reflection: It is quite remarkable that Queen Margaret learned to compartmentalize chaos. Undoubtedly, her personal world had its fair share of trauma. Yet, she obviously established boundaries on her reactions so that it could not negatively invade all other areas of her life. She gave chaos and confusion boundaries to make room for peace. Queen, that's a whole message all by itself. We truly can go through something without allowing that something to go through us..

Note to
self ~

QUEEN, YOU BETTER REACH FOR HELP WHEN YOU NEED IT.

QUEEN, YOU ARE THE ANSWER TO SOMEBODY'S PRAYER.

DAY 22: ADDING BLISS TO HAPPINESS
Insights from Queen Anna, Hungary; 1531

Today's Affirmation: I take ownership of creating happiness in my own world. I hold space for harmony, love, and peace among those to whom I am connected. I am a recipient of much love. I am giver of much love.

Scripture: If it is possible, as far as it depends on you, live at peace with everyone. *Romans 12:18*

The eldest daughter in her family, Anna was also considered her father's favorite child. Similarly, although she was the 4th wife of her husband King Philip, Anna was reportedly her husband's most beloved wife. An affinity to be loved seemed to follow her presence.

Atypical to her time, Queen Anna's marriage to King Philip is described as happy. According to diplomats, the king was in love with his young bride. Astoundingly, there are no records of Philip having mistresses during the time of their marriage. It is believed that Philip and Anna existed in a relationship of mutual respect and goodwill towards one another. In fact, their marriage broke the cultural norms of its time. In a world full of marriages complete with mistresses and emptiness, King Philip is reputed as deeply devoted to Queen Anne with regular displays of affection and romance. Yes sis, this type of commitment does still exist!

Adding bliss to happiness, Philip and Anna's marriage had been arranged to provide the king with a male heir to the throne. What joy filled the castle when Anna gave birth to five children, among which were four sons. Although the three eldest sons died before Philip, the youngest remained alive and eventually succeeded to the throne as King Phillip III.

Lastly, in the same way that she seemed to receive love with ease, Queen Anna gave love just as easily. She was described as a good stepmother to Philip's daughters. Queen Anna was also depicted as vivid and cheerful, and managed to ease up some of the stiff atmosphere at the Spanish court by exuding care that was genuine for others.

Reflection: Queen Anna loved and gave love generously. She experienced happiness in her marriage and blended family. Defying stereotypes, she largely created cheer and joy in her own world. Queen, I am sending so much love your way, love to the overflow. May we give love, may we receive love bountifully!

Note to
self ~

DAY 23: SURVIVOR

Insights from Queen Elisabeth, France; 1570

Today's Affirmation: I declare that my moral compass is intact. I am rooted and grounded in a deep conviction regarding what is good and right in this world. My actions are aligned with goodness toward humanity throughout all of my days.

Scripture: He that loves not, knows not God, for God is love. *1 John 4:8*

Although eight of her siblings died in infancy, Elisabeth of Austria survived as the fifth child and second daughter of her parents' sixteen children. Man, sis came into this world with a whole testimony! But, it did not stop there. She kept winning!

With her flawless white skin, long blond hair and perfect physique, she was considered one of the great beauties of the era. She was also intellectually talented. It is reported that her brothers were educated before her; yet the curious princess soon joined and even overshadowed them in their studies.

After Elisabeth and her future husband, King Charles IX of France, were formally married, the new queen officially entered Paris four days later. Subsequently, she disappeared from all public life. Eventually her husband, King Charles, realized that the liberal ways of the French Court might have shocked Elisabeth. So, along with his mother, he tried to do a better job of shielding her from its excesses.

Because the ways of the French were so foreign to her sheltered upbringing, Queen Elisabeth felt lonely in the lively and dissolute French court. To occupy herself, she flourished in embroidery work, reading, and the practice of charitable service projects.

The queen observed mass twice daily. Despite her strong opposition to Protestantism, she was horrified by the news that thousands of Protestants were murdered in Paris. Elisabeth managed to assure a promise to spare the lives of the foreign Protestants. Unlike other prominent Catholics, she did not publicly rejoice at their deaths.

Reflection: Queen Elisabeth's love for humanity was stronger than her allegiance to a particular religion. She refused to be silently complicit in wrong actions but instead used her platform to stand for good. Be your brave self, queen!

Note to self ~

DAY 24: HER MOTHER'S DAUGHTER

Insights from Athaliah, Queen of Judah; 842 BC

Today's Affirmation: I willingly exchange my thoughts for the thoughts of Christ. My mind is being renewed to reflect His mindset daily. Today, I think Christ-like thoughts and govern myself accordingly.

Scripture: Do not conform to the pattern of this world but be transformed by the renewing of your mind. Then you will be able to test and approve what God's will is - His good, pleasing and perfect will. *Romans 12:2*

Upon hearing that her own son, King Ahaziah, was dead, this scheming mother used the moment of grief throughout the land to usurp the power of the throne. Being the offspring of wicked Queen Jezebel, it's no surprise that this daughter seemingly inherited her mother's reproachable ways. She placed assassination targets on the backs of all the royal descendants of the house of Judah. She imputed innocent bloodshed, deep grief, and relentless anguish among her own countrymen. Countless other mothers, at the hands of this opportunist mother, wept for the loss of their own children.

Many feared that Queen Athaliah's mean-spirited efforts to obtain the throne would not even spare her own grandchild, the next heir to the throne. Ahaziah's sister rescued her nursing nephew and hid him in the care of his nursemaid. He was in hiding with them in the house of God for six years while Queen Athaliah reigned over the land.

"Long live the king," the people sang and cheered when the son of the deceased king was revealed. When Athaliah heard the noise of the guards and of the people, she came to check out the commotion. She looked and behold, standing by the pillar was the young king. Then Athaliah tore her clothes and cried, "Treason! Treason!" Jehoiada the priest commanded that she be brought forth and later put to death. It's ironic that after her mass massacre of innocent lives to secure the throne, she reaped her own actions and loss the throne regardless.

Reflection: Is there anything that I desire so badly that my heart flirts with thoughts of inappropriate behavior to obtain it? Have I brought every thought and plan subject to the word of God?

Note to
self ~

I
BID YOU
INNER PEACE.

QUEEN, SOMETIMES "NO" IS THE PERFECT ANSWER.

DAY 25: CROSSFIRE

Insights from Bathsheba, Queen of Israel

Today's Affirmation: I declare that my life is free from the residue of negative choices made by others. Moving forward, my life will be reflective of having mercy and grace follow me all my days. I go forward in my renewed state and clean start.

Scripture: And the Lord will restore to you the years that the locust hath eaten, the cankerworm, and the caterpillar, and the palmerworm, my great army which I sent among you. *Joel 2:25*

Caught in the crossfires of another's schemes, Bathsheba has historically suffered the accusations of being a seducer of sorts, bathing within the gaze of the king's eye. But Queen listen, contextual studies reveal that her actions were not beyond the norm of cultural practices during that time. Both in factual and cultural terms, Bathsheba was simply a woman taking her regular bath. She became the target of a king's desire to have and add her to his cohort of wives and concubines.

Meanwhile, Bathsheba was the wife of a soldier, Uriah the Hittite. He was often out in the fields of war and thus, she spent many days as sole caretaker of their home. Her marriage included the sacrificial giving of her husband, - both his time and energy - to the well-being of the country. This same wife, unaware of the plot of the king, later became a grieving widow when the love of her beloved spouse was murdered.

Bathsheba birthed several children including the full-term birth and subsequent death of the unnamed infant son of King David. This precious child lost his young life as divine punishment for his father's choices. This mother certainly mourned the loss of the fruit of her womb. Due to choices beyond her own, Bathsheba suffered deep heartaches several times over in various areas of her life. After sovereign consequences were lifted, Bathsheba, now wed to King David, gave birth to her beloved son Solomon. This son became known as the wisest man who ever lived.

Reflection: Bathsheba's inability to explain her suffering and shame without exposing the true culprit was possibly limited. She has been ill reputed for choices that were beyond her own making. Has another's person's poor choices ever impacted your life? Have you ever had to take the negative wrap for something that was beyond your control? Have you made room for the Father's redemptive grace to restore your loss to you?

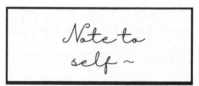

DAY 26: DESTINED TO BE A STAR
Insights from Esther, Queen of Persia; 478 BC

Today's Affirmation: God chooses whom He chooses. I trust His choice of me. Today, I will walk boldly into every opportunity that His selection affords me.

Scripture: Then Peter began to speak: "I now truly understand that God does not show favoritism, but welcomes those from every nation who fear Him and do what is right." *Acts 10: 34-35*

In alignment with the meaning of her name, Esther seemed destined to be a star, the star in fact of her family, of her people, of a nation. Still living in exile in an foreign land, we can only imagine the thoughts that must have run through the mind of this niece, being raised as a daughter under the loving eye of an uncle. Life was unfolding with its interesting turns and twists. Unusual events began to occur in the Persian Kingdom which created unexpected opportunities for promotion for this beautiful orphan maiden.

Angered by his former queen's refusal to come out and be viewed, (more likely gawked at,but we chat it out about her on a different day) by he and his guests, Ahasuerus, king of the Persian land, was on a quest to secure a new heiress for the throne. Maidens gathered from all across the land with hopes that they might catch the king's eye and in doing so secure the crown and title Queen of Persia.

The grooming process weaned out some candidates and promoted others as they squared off shoulder to shoulder to battle for this coveted position. Fortunately, under her uncle's careful guidance, Esther found herself on the short list of potentials.

Reflection: Nobody knew better than Esther that not a single thing about her lineage indicated that she was qualified to be the next queen of Persia. Yet, when the doors of opportunity opened, she did not limit herself but instead walked through committedly. She embraced the familiar passage that she was created for "such a time as this." You too Queen, you too have been created for "such a time as this" in your personal world of influence and community. Will you walk through the open door? My oldest girlfriend often says, "God does not open the door just to leave you standing in the hallway. He brings us into our blessing all the way!" Go all the way sis.

> Note to
> self ~

DAY 27: SOWING AND REAPING

Insights from Jezebel, Queen of Israel

Today's Affirmation: Today, I receive grace for past decisions that would have resulted in undesirable consequences for my life. Today, I live very conscious of the decisions that I make and their impact on my life as well as the lives of others. Moving forward, I sow good seeds only.

Scripture: Be not deceived; God is not mocked. For whatsoever a man soweth, that shall he also reap. *Galatians 6:7*

Jezebel, already a princess by birthright, slid into a royalty slot again when she married the king of Israel. This man loved her so much that he went against his own religious background to take her as his wife. As a former princess who never gave up her idolatrous religion, Matrimony with Queen Jezebel's was stock full of clashes between her gods and that of her husband's - the one, true living God.

Queen Jezebel's reputation swept across the countryside. She was known to be manipulative, evil, hurtful and hateful, and excessively cruel. Most importantly, she was one of the most unrestrained persecutors of the saints as a direct antagonist to her husband's religion. As a nod to her heathen worship, she positioned four hundred and fifty false prophets to push her agenda of infiltrating the land with teachings on Baal. Her conduct was very disastrous to the kingdom in which she reigned.

Jezebel eventually reaped what she had sown. As someone who was known for her cruel actions, her chambermaids eventually threw her out of a window. She was dashed in pieces on the street; horses walked over her body, and ultimately, she was eaten by dogs on the ground where she lay. Her name became synonymous with a wicked woman. To this day, calling a woman by Queen Jezebel's name holds an unmistakably negative connotation.

Reflection: She sowed it. She reaped it. I am sowing it. I will reap it. Am I sowing what I desire to reap?

Note to
self ~

BOUNDARIES
ARE
BEAUTIFUL.
QUEEN,
HONOR YOURS.

QUEEN,
ROYALTY
IS WHO YOU
ARE.

DAY 28: NO

Insights from Vashti, Queen of Persia

Today's Affirmation: Today, I walk in the healthy boundaries that are established for my life. I refuse to accept less than what makes me well. I declare safe spaces all throughout my life. In Jesus' name.

Scripture: God is within her; she will not fall; God will help her at break of day. *Psalm 46:5*

She said, "No!" And listen sis, she meant it.
In a culture and time during which women were expected to obey, that "no" shifted her entire status and forever impacted her life.

Queen Vashti, the infamous first wife of King Ahasuerus in the Book of Esther, refused to appear at the king's banquet when summoned to be viewed by his guests. Scripture records that on the 7th day of the feast, when the king's heart was merry with wine, he desired that his wife put on her royal crown and come to be admired by his guests - more specifically the many male guests whose hearts were also merry with wine! When the chambermaids went to escort her to the room, they returned empty-handed. Again, Queen Vashti had said no. She meant it.

Given the times in which she lived, the king's expectations would not have come as much of a surprise, yet Queen Vashti denied his wishes.

Her refusal to come to the banquet at the king's command undeniably would have its share of consequences. A deeper look into the story reveals that the punishment escalated to banishment because of the the other husbands who witnessed what happened at the feast. In fear that their wives would follow the queen's lead, they urged the King to to make an example out of Queen Vashti. The husbands' aim was that the King's punishment would break other women who were perhaps watching and would possibly be emboldened to replicate a freedom to choose not to participate in certain activities when summoned by their husbands, especially if that request was belittling or perhaps unsafe for them.

Reflection: How Queen Vashti gained the courage to say no, to have a personal standard even when it came to the king, we may never know. However, she did, and accepted the results. Perhaps, she knew in heart, regardless of what happened, she would be okay. She understood that some things were simply unacceptable for her life. Have you determined your non-negotiable "no"? Are you clear about the parts of yourself that are absolutely, regardless of the cost, not for sell, entertainment, nor manipulation by others?

Note to
self ~

DAY 29: BOLD MOVES

Insights from Empress Elisabeth of Austria and Hungary

Today's Affirmation: Today, I put aside all worry regarding who is not for me. Instead I choose to walk in peace, knowing that my steps are ordered by the Lord. He is bringing it to me. Or, He is bringing me to it. Either way, it is well.

Scripture: The steps of a good man are ordered by the Lord: and he delights in his way. *Psalms 37:23*

The domineering mother of 23-year-old Emperor Franz Joseph, preferred to have a niece as a daughter-in-law instead of a complete stranger. At any cost, they were always careful about safeguarding who would get to sit on that thronet! As such, good ole' mother attempted to arrange a marriage between her son and her sister's eldest daughter, Helene. Although the couple had never met, this mother was sure that her son would obey her wishes and do just as she commanded. Without further ado, she invited her sister and niece to receive a formal marriage proposal in Upper Austria. Trailing along, Elisabeth made the journey with her family as well.

Because the family had recently grieved the loss of a family member, they were all dressed in ceremonial black attire when they arrived for the visit. It is reputed that while black was not the most becoming choice for the eldest sister, it was flattering for the younger maiden

Elisabeth. At once, the son, intended to be engaged to the elder sister, was smitten by his younger cousin.

In a bold move against his authoritative mother, the young gentleman did not request the hand of the older sister in marriage but instead expressed his love for the younger one. He refused to propose to Helene as expected. Instead he defied his mother and informed her that if Elisabeth could not be his beloved, he would forego marriage completely. An engagement announcement went out five days later. In an additional eight months, the couple united in holy matrimony!

Reflection: Regardless of man's schemes, interventions, and efforts, what was destined for Queen Elisabeth became hers. Another person's preference could not thwart what lay in store for her to receive. Likewise you and I queen, likewise us!

Note to
self ~

DAY 30: VICTORY BEFORE WAR

Insights from Queen Kandake, Egypt - Part Two

Today's Affirmation: Because His reputation goes before me, today I will experience victories that He has already won. In every area of my life, I triumph because the ultimate Champion has fought on my behalf.

Scripture: Through You, we will push back our adversaries; Through Your name, we will trample down those who revolt against us. *Psalm 44:5*

Because she is deserving of a little bit more of her story. Yes, this is the same Queen Kandake from day nineteen. Of her throes with Alexander the Great, it is largely reputed that the knees of this undefeated ruler buckled when he chanced upon an encounter with Queen Candace.

Queen Kandake, legend has it, gathered her troops and lined them up across a long divide in the intersection of Alexander's war path. Then she stood on a throne which was mounted on top of two African Elephants, and waited for Alexander to show up. This undefeated warrior, having already heard of the queen's combative prowess. He calculated the odds of capturing a victory against this embolden queen. standing on the backs of her elephants, with majestic troops bringing up the rear. Alexander had no desire to take his first loss, especially at the hands of a woman. Instead of continuing forward, he surveyed the scene, pulled back his troops, and made a turn-around back towards his own territory.

A different recounting summarizes that in an off the record meeting, a few options were presented to Alexander by Queen Kandake. He could either leave her region immediately or stay the course with his invasion. As a result, he would have his head cut off and rolled down a hill as part of her victory. Whether it was the caravan of troops in his path or their conversations in private, Queen Kandake secured another victory via her winning reputation. Her track record was enough to defeat this enemy.

Reflection: Queen Kandake won battles before she even entered a fight. Victories came simply at the mention of her name. Her reputation, one that she had duly earned, had a positive impact on her life. And there is a confidence that we too can have in a reputation sis! Perhaps not our own, but that of the Greater One! Take a look at our confession for today.

Note to
self ~

DAY 31: WIN-WIN

Insights from Queen of Sheba (no name recorded); 1555

Today's Affirmation: I will show up in this world fully representing the magnificence that lives on the inside of me. My light will shine at its full capacity as I walk in all that God has destined for my life. Even when requesting assistance to meet a need, I will display His glory that forever shines over my life.

Scripture: I will sing to the Lord because he has dealt bountifully with me. *Psalm 13:6*

As he worked at rebuilding the temple, King Solomon sought to buy the best materials for esteemed construction project from merchants throughout the world. It is believed that one of his trade encounters was with Tamrin, a representative from an area within the land of Ethiopia, whose ruler was the Queen of Sheba.

It is recounted that when Tamrin returned to Ethiopia, he told the queen of the extravagant opulence that he had witnessed in Jerusalem. He shared details of Solomon's insight and anointed wisdom. With great interest in such details, the Queen of Sheba determined that she would experience Solomon's kingdom for herself. I agree! Sometimes, you have see things with your own eyes.

In full representation of her own accomplishments, the Queen of Sheba came to Jerusalem bearing gifts that are noted as unsurpassed to this day. While she certainly desired something from King Solomon - to inquire of him the hard questions - she was also fully capable of contributing to him. This postured their exchange as mutually beneficial. At the closure of their connection, both parties experienced increase. It is recorded that in addition to being able to receive, the Queen of Sheba was able to give to King Solomon riches beyond any other guests, prior and yet to come.

Reflection: When the Queen of Sheba arrived with a request for King Solomon, the splendor of what she brought to the table in their exchange could not be denied. Its grandeur has not been surpassed in history. She did not shrink in his presence but represented herself with excellence beyond compare. Queens, may we too always know the value that we bring to the table!

Note to
self ~

SHINE NOW QUEEN. RIGHT NOW.

WHEN
CONSIDERING ALL
THINGS THAT MATTER,
INCLUDE YOURSELF.

ABOUT THE AUTHOR

Her life passion, empowering others, is at the core of Gena L. Jerkins. Ed. D service within the education, humanitarian, and philanthropic arenas. She has garnered over 20+ impactful years of combined service in the public, collegiate, and private education sectors. Her role as classroom teacher, middle school assistant. principal, and principal within the public-school system offered years of valuable engagement with staff, students, parents and stakeholders alike. Her tenure in higher education as Student and First Year Teacher Supervisor, Adjunct Professor, Guest Facilitator, and Teacher Trainer intertwined with current consulting, facilitating, and professional development engagements continue to strengthen her knowledgeable matriculation in the field. Dr. Jerkins also adds depth to her perspective on education via international explorations in both the Honduras and Kenya, Africa educational settings. Combining the aforementioned with volunteerism in empowerment settings have informed her enriched perspective and practices in the field of education.

Dr. Jerkins holds a Bachelor of Art with Teacher certification as well as Master of Curriculum and Instruction with an emphasis in multicultural studies from Texas A&M University. Her doctorate in Educational Leadership and Administration is from the University of Houston. As a lifelong scholar, she recently obtained a Master of Arts in Christian Leadership from Dallas Theological Seminary. Her additional endorsements include current Mid-Management and Superintendent certifications.

Of note, Dr. Jerkins also serves as founder and executive director of Refresh Lam Moi (2012), a 501c3 organization which exists to empower women to reset the rhythm of their own lives. While it may be different for each person, the organization envisions women living their absolute best lives. www.MYREFRESHLAMMOI.org

You are able to connect with Dr. Jerkins via info@drgenalyn.com. Her website is www.DRGENALYN.com

Follow DRGENALYN on the following social media platforms:

Facebook

Instagram

Youtube

Twitter

TicTok

Snapchat

SOURCE ACKNOWLEDGEMENT

*Wikipedia served as the primary source of general historical details. As mentioned in the author's note, for additional facts on the lives of these queens and others beyond this compilation, it is recommended to utilize resources available online for more in-depth research.

Made in USA - Kendallville, IN
33501_9798583183692
06.27.2022 1321